EXPERIMENTS with WEATHER

Contents

What Makes the Weather?

A blanket of air surrounds the earth like a transparent shell. This is called the atmosphere. It gives us oxygen to breathe and keeps the earth's temperature at just the right level.

Weather is described in terms of variable conditions such as temperature, humidity, wind velocity, precipitation and barometric pressure. In fact, air is where the weather is. But it takes more than air to make weather.

The state of the air or atmosphere with respect to heat or cold and other meterological phenomena form the weather. Weather changes from hour to hour, day to day, season to season and place to place. It occurs on Earth primarily in the troposphere, or lower atmosphere, and is driven by energy from the Sun and the rotation of the Earth.

Cactus in Arizona

Snow in mountains

Did you know?

The atmosphere stretches far above the ground, but weather changes occur only in the lower 9.6 kilometres.

Air and Weather

Air is all around us. It is a mixture of gases. It is colourless, odourless, tasteless, gaseous mixture of mainly O_2 and nitrogen with lesser amounts of argon, CO_2, hydorgen, etc. and has no smell. It is really a mixture of different gases. We cannot see air but we can feel it when the wind blows. We also know that air has weight.

Find out for yourself that there is air

You will need:

- an empty bottle
- a bowl of water

1. Turn the bottle upside down.
2. Then push it straight down into the pan containing water. What do you see? No water enters the bottle because the bottle is full of air.
3. Tilt the bottle and the air will rush out. Only then will the water move into the bottle.

What is air composed of?

Air is made up of invisible gases. The main gas is nitrogen and then come oxygen and argon. There is also some water vapour in the air unless it is very dry.

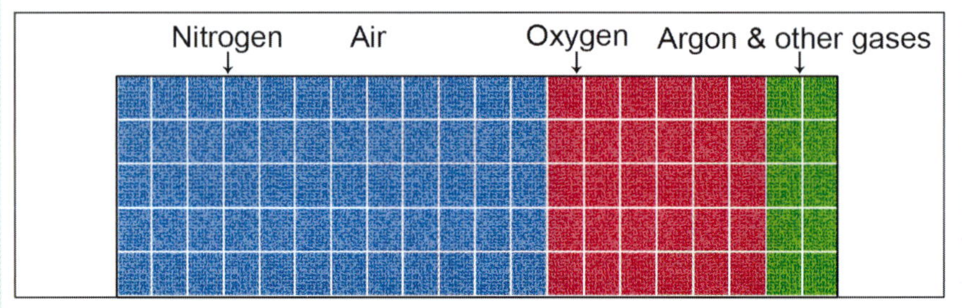

The gases in the air are in the form of very tiny particles called *molecules*. A molecule is the smallest part of a substance that retains the nature of the substance. Air molecules are like pingpong balls that are too small to be seen. They move about in space in a random way and bounce a lot.

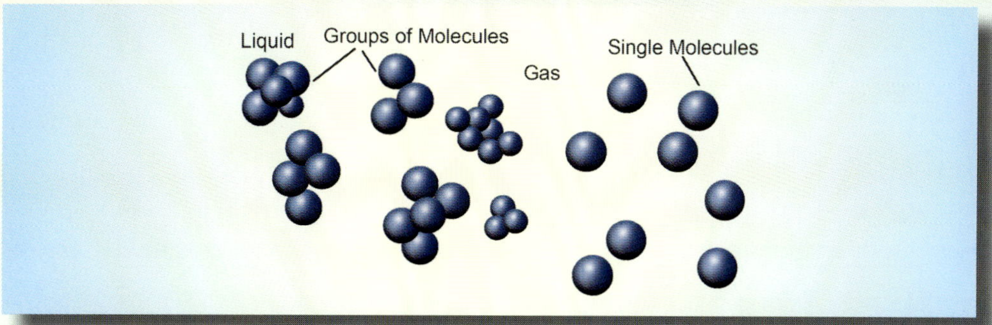

Air has weight

Air is heavier than you think. An average roomful of air weighs more than 45 kg. All this air presses down on the ground just like any solid object.

See it for yourself.

You will need:

- a metre stick
- thread
- two bulldog clips
- two balloons

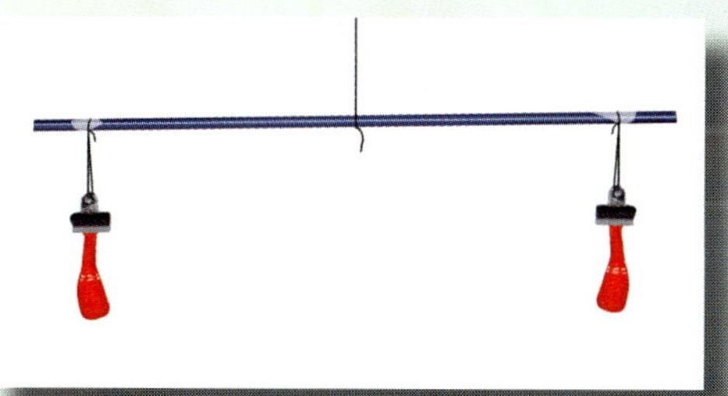

1. Hang the stick at its mid-point by a piece of thread.
2. Hang the bulldog clips at the two ends of the stick and attach the balloons, as shown in the picture.
3. Slide the clips to obtain a balance.
4. Ask a friend to hold the stick while you carefully remove one balloon and blow it up.
5. Tie the balloon at its neck and hang it back in its place.
6. Check what happens when your friend lets go of the balance.

Air has pressure

The weight of the air presses against the earth in all directions. This push of the air is called pressure. For example, if you stand at the sea level, the air in the atmosphere will be pressing down on you with a weight equal to that of a big car. However, you do not feel this because the air inside your body has its own pressure, pressing outward. The two balance each other out so that you remain comfortable.

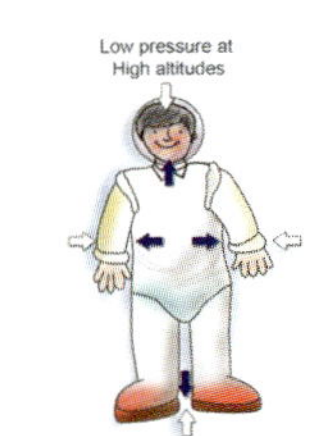

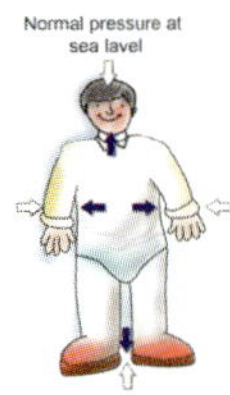

You can feel the air pressure

1. Take a plunger which we normally use to clear blocked drains.
2. Press it on to the floor.
3. Now try to pull it up.

Plunger

What happens?

You find it hard to pull it up. The air was pushed out from the cup when you pushed the plunger down. The outside air now presses on the cup and holds it to the ground.

Air pressure can be measured

The instrument used for measuring air pressure is called a *barometer*. The commonest kind is known as an aneroid barometer. It has a drum from which almost all the air has been removed (creating a near vacuum). Changes in air pressure make the drum expand or contract, which causes the pointer to move around the dial. Clear and settled weather is likely when the pressure is high. Low pressure indicates unsettled and stormy weather.

Make your own barometer

A barometer can show changes in air pressure.

You will need:

- an empty glass jar
- a sheet of rubber obtained from a balloon
- a rubber band
- a drinking straw
- a pin

1. Fasten a piece of thin rubber sheet over the top of the jar with a rubber band.
2. Glue the drinking straw to the stretched rubber sheet.
3. Glue the pin to the other end of the straw.
4. Make a chart and place it behind your barometer. Mark the position of the pin every hour.

What happens?

Air presses down on the stretched balloon. A change in the pressure makes the straw move. Your chart will show how much it moves.

What causes high and low pressure

Air pressure changes from place to place and from time to time in the same place. These changes are sometimes caused by changes in temperature.
When the sun's heat warms the air, its molecules are far apart. Warm air weighs less than cold air, therefore it pushes less against the earth or exerts a low pressure. When the air is cooler, its molecules are close together and that makes it heavier. It pushes with more weight and thus exerts a high pressure.

Heat and Weather

The most important 'cause' of weather is the heating and cooling of air. Heat causes winds. It is also responsible for the different ways in which water vapour appears in the atmosphere.

Heat from the sun warms the land and the water. The warm land and water then warm the air.

The air around the earth moves because it is heated by the sun. The warm air rises upwards and cold air flows into its place.

You can see how hot air rises by watching a hot air balloon. To go higher, the balloonist turns up the gas flame to warm the air inside the balloon. To go lower, the balloonist turns down the flame so that the air in the balloon cools down.

See it for yourself

Through simple experiments you can find out how heat warms the land, the water and the air.

You will need:

- 2 pans
- some sand or soil
- some water
- 2 thermometers

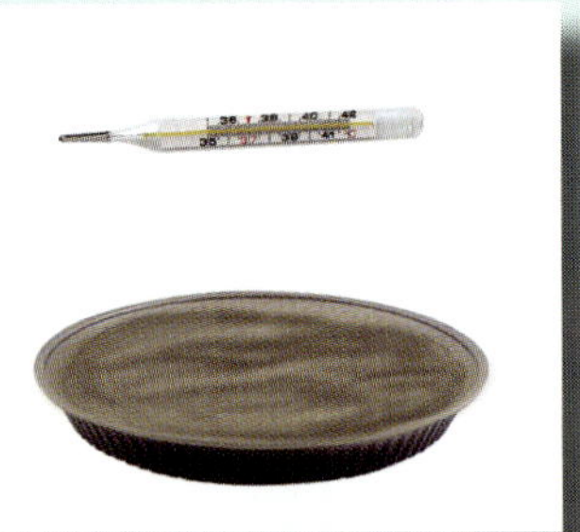

1. Take two empty pans of the same size.
2. Fill each of the pans with the same amount of soil or sand.
3. Set one pan in the sunshine and the other in the shade. Leave them there for two hours.
4. Then take the temperature of the soil in each pan. What do you see? Are the temperatures the same? How much do they differ?
5. Now empty the pans and dry them.
6. Then fill each of them with the same amount of fresh water.

7. Set one pan in the sunshine and the other in the shade. Leave them there for two hours.
8. Now note the temperature of the water in both the pans.

What do you observe? Is the temperature the same in both the pans? How much does it differ?

What is the temperature today?

You will need:

- 2 thermometers
- a watch
- a sheet of paper
- a pen

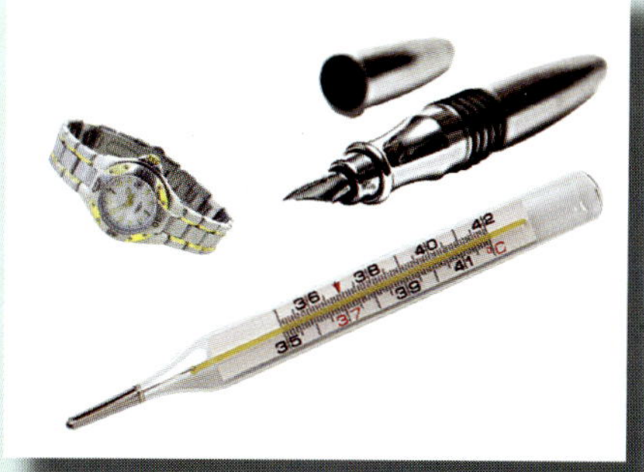

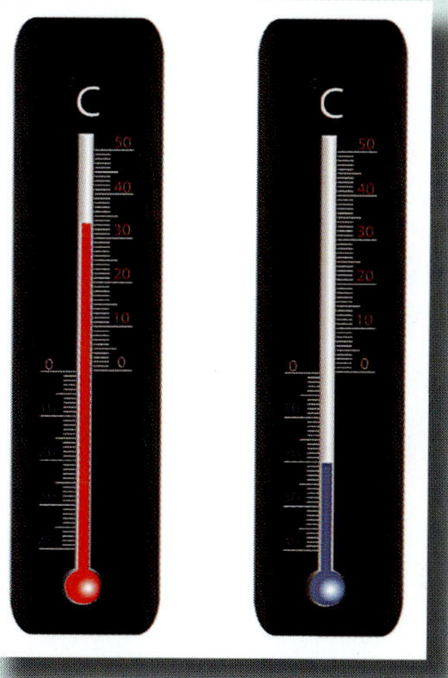

1. Obtain two thermometers. Hang one in the sunshine and the other in the shade.
2. Note the readings every hour. Write down the temperatures you read on two different charts. Do this for two or three days.
3. Now study the temperatures you have noted. Do you see the difference in the two charts? At what time of the day was it the warmest? When was it the coldest? What do you conclude?

Wind and Weather

Whenever air is heated, it expands. This makes it lighter, and light air rises. As the warm air rises, cooler air flows in to take its place. This movement of air is called *wind*. Wind is simply air in motion.

Winds are an important part of our weather. You will appreciate it more when you look at the pictures given below.

Light Breeze

Moderate Wind

Strong Wind

Storm

Hurricane

Wind patterns

Different parts of the earth receive different amounts of heat. Near the equator, the sun is overhead and heats the earth intensely. Near the poles, the sun's rays strike the earth at a low angle and so the heat is not so intense.

Winds, caused by the hot air rising upwards from tropical equator region and the cold air flowing from the earth's frozen regions into this space, flow in regular patterns. The streams of cool air are called *trade winds*.

The *land* and *sea breezes* also follow a regular pattern.

The *land* is heated to a higher temperature than the sea during the day. Air over the land becomes warmer and rises, and cool air from the sea takes its place. So in the daytime there is a breeze blowing towards the land.

At night, the land cools down faster than the sea. So there is a breeze in the opposite direction.

Land and sea breezes can also be seasonal. Then they are called the *Monsoons*. The monsoons bring rain.

Useful winds

Wind may be useful to us. It can help dry clothes hanging on the line. It can turn windmills. It can push sailboats through water.

Harmful winds

However, there are harmful winds also. Tornadoes and hurricanes, for example, are very strong and dangerous winds.

Hurricanes are powerful swirling masses of cyclonic wind, clouds and rain that begin over the warm tropical oceans and move westward, dying out as they reach the land. Hurricanes are the cyclones that occur in the West Indies. In the Pacific they are called *typhoons*.

Hurricanes are the deadliest storms on the earth. They can wash away entire beaches, sink boats, pull trees right out of the ground and kill people.

Cyclones are heavy storms with the wind forming a spiral around a centre. Cyclones occur in low-pressure areas and may extend over an area half the size of India. They travel at very high speeds.

Tropical cyclones are severe cyclones that occur in the tropics, where ocean waters give them energy.

Cyclones have different names depending upon where they originate!

Tornadoes are concentrated funnel shaped cyclonic storms caused by hot air spinning as it rises upwards. They can move at speeds of more than 300 mph and can suck up everything in their path.

Measuring Wind Directions and Wind Speed

We can measure wind directions and wind speeds. Windvanes show wind directions. Anemometers are used to measure wind speeds.

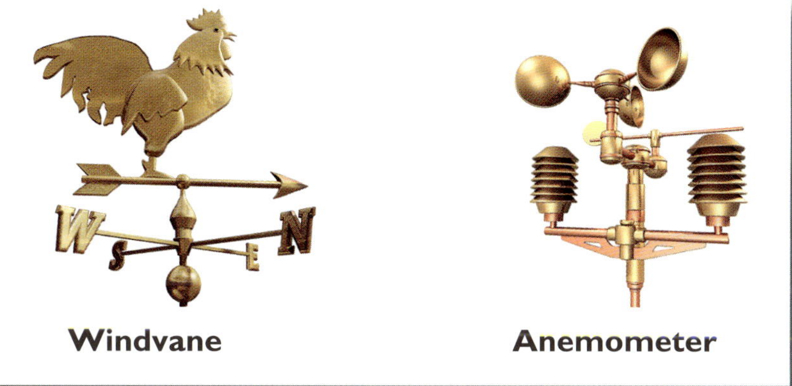

Windvane Anemometer

Make your own windvane

You can make your own windvane at home.

You will need:
- a strong card
- a pencil
- a pair of scissors
- plastic drinking straws
- glue
- a tall plastic bottle
- sand
- a long thin rod
- a rubber band
- a compass needle

1. Draw a windvane on the card. Cut it out.
2. Glue a straw to the centre of the vane.
3. Fix the pencil at right angles to the rod with the rubber band, so that it forms a cross.

4. Fill the bottle with sand, and stick the rod into the sand.
5. Write N on a square piece of card and stick it to the pencil.
6. Place a small piece of drinking straw on the rod so that it rests on the crossbar.
7. Place the wind-vane on the rod. It should turn freely.
8. Take your wind-vane outside. With the help of the compass, find out which way North is. Position your wind-vane so that N points towards North. The direction of the vane will give you the direction of the wind.

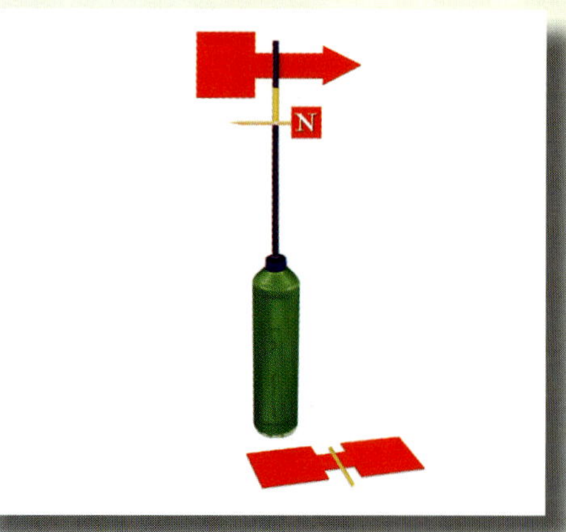

Make your own anemometer

You can make your own anemometer and find out how fast the wind is blowing.

You will need:

- 4 empty ice cream cups
- paper and glue
- red and green paint and a brush
- 3 thin, 25 cm long wooden sticks
- a tall plastic bottle filled with sand
- a cork, a round bead and a pin

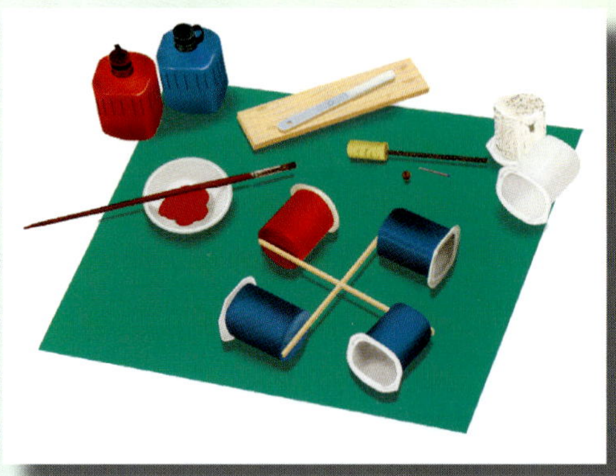

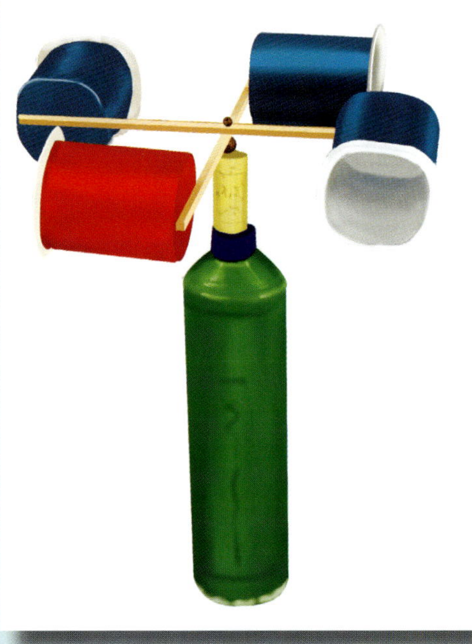

1. Staple the handles of the four paper cups to the edge of the plate. (If the cups are without handles, you can fix your own. Cut them out from a thin cardboard sheet.)
2. Put the long pin into the top of the thin stick or the long pencil.
3. Cut a hole in the paper plate.
4. Slip the plate over the pin.
5. Place your anemometer in the wind. Now watch it go round.
6. Note how many times it goes round in a minute.

Water Vapour and Weather

Air molecules are close together when the air is cool. So they move slowly. They move faster and are farther apart when the air is warm. Then there is room for other things. That is how dust and molecules of water get accommodated into the air.

How does water get into the air?

The sun heats the oceans, rivers and lakes. Heat makes the molecules of water move faster and separate from one another. They move into the air. When this happens we say that the water evaporates. The water is now called water vapour.

Water evaporates from oceans, rivers and lakes. It also evaporates from the ground and from the plants. All air contains water vapour.

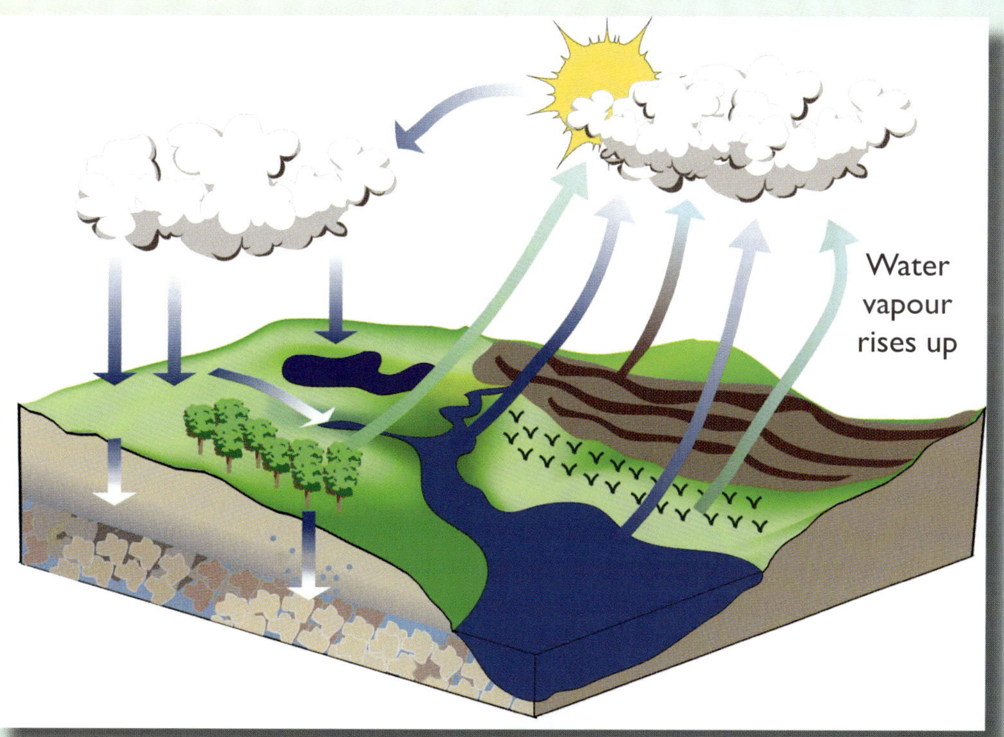

You can find out how water gets into the air

You will need:

- 2 empty pans of the same size
- some water

1. Fill the two pans with water up to about half an inch from the bottom.
2. Now leave one pan in the shade.
3. Set the other pan in sunshine.
4. Watch them every day. What do you observe?

The water in both the pans disappears. But the water kept in the sunshine disappears faster.

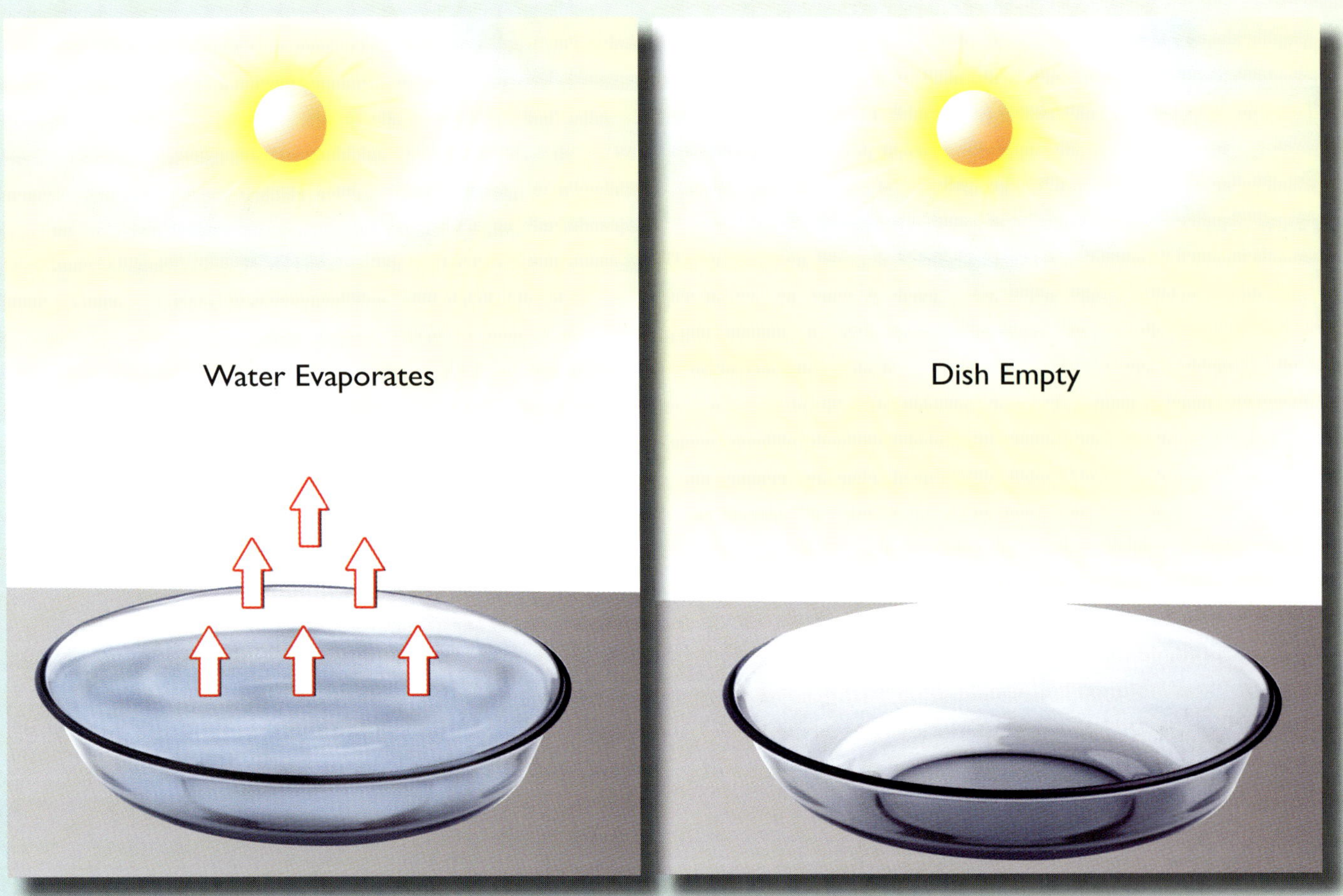

Humidity

The amount of water vapour present in the air is called *humidity*. On days when there is a lot of water vapour in the air, you feel sultry and humid. High humidity is often accompanied by rain.

The instrument used to measure humidity is called a *hygrometer*.

Make your own hygrometer

You will need:

- a wooden stand
- a cotton reel
- a drinking straw
- a long human hair
- a board pin
- a card
- sellotape

1. Fix the cotton reel to the wooden board as shown in the picture.
2. Fix a long human hair to the top of the stand with the sellotape.
3. Carefully run the hair over the reel.

4. Stick the card to the stand under the reel.
5. Pin one end of the straw to the card and tie the hair near the end.

An interesting fact

The hair will be longer when there is water vapour in the air than when the air is dry. As the humidity changes, the hair will stretch or shrink, moving the straw either up or down.

Why it rains?

As water vapour rises up into the atmosphere, it cools down and changes back, or condenses, into droplets of water.

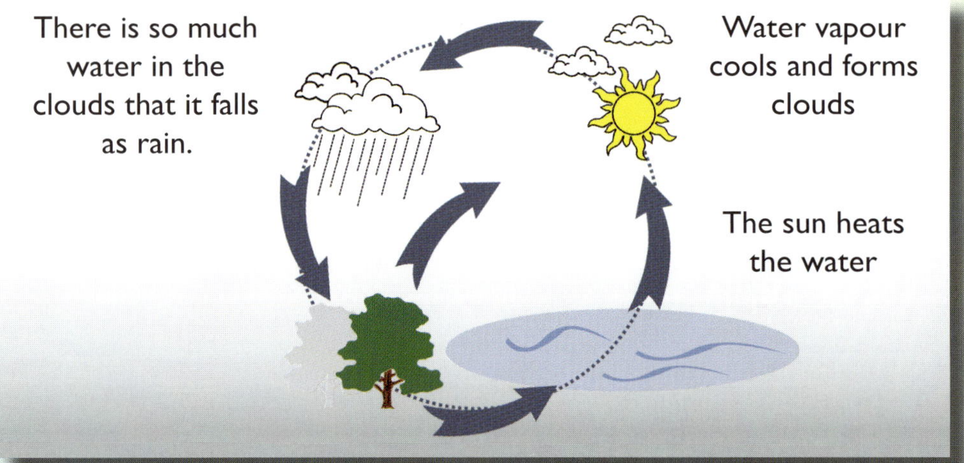

You can turn water vapour into drops

What happens to water vapour as it rises, can be made to happen right inside your house.

You will need:

- an empty glass
- some ice cubes
- a bowl
- a small piece of board
- some water

1. Fill the empty glass with water and ice cubes.
2. Take a bowl and fill it with warm water.
3. Now place the board over the bowl and set the glass over the bowl.

The water vapour in the air will form drops on the cold glass. The drops will soon run down on the outer surface of the glass.

The water molecules after condensing slow down and come together. Water gathers around tiny specks of dust and salt in the air to form larger water droplets. Gradually, the droplets gather together to form a *cloud* in the sky.

Clouds

Clouds are very tiny droplets of condensed water vapour, so small that they do not have enough weight to fall to the Earth, and hence float around in the air. In simple words, a cloud is a visible mass of water droplets or frozen crystals suspended in the atmosphere above the surface of the Earth. At first they are white and gauzy. As they become heavy with water, they become thick and grey. Finally the droplets become so heavy that they clump together and fall to the earth. If the temperature is high enough they come down as *rain*. Otherwise they land as *hail* or *snow*.

Different types of clouds

There are three main types of clouds.

1. Cirriform (detached and whispy): are found at high altitude, above 20,000 feet. These are composed of ice crystals and actually appear to be white and transparent.
2. Cumuliform (rolled or rippled): It is a convective cloud with vertical development formed by rising air currents in unstable air.
3. Stratiform: continuous layers in sheets.

Make your own cloud

You will need:

- a glass jar, with a mouth big enough for your fist to go in
- a sheet of rubber obtained from slitting a large balloon
- some chalk dust
- a strong rubber band

1. Pour water into the jar up to about an inch from the bottom.
2. Place the rubber sheet over the mouth of the jar.
3. Keep it in place with some heavy object like a book. Leave it covered for ten minutes.
4. Now lift the rubber sheet and put the chalk dust into the jar.
5. Quickly secure the rubber sheet tightly over the mouth of the jar with the rubber band.

6. Push your fist against the rubber sheet until it is inside the jar. This will warm the air inside the jar and make it hold more water vapour.
7. After ten seconds, remove your fist quickly. This will suddenly cool the air in the jar. Cold air holds less water vapour than warm air. The extra water will condense around the chalk particles. As a result, a cloud will form inside the jar.

Measuring rain

Rain is measured by an instrument called the *rain gauge*. The depth of water that collects in the rain gauge is used to measure the rainfall. It is measured in millimetres.

Rain Gauge

Make your own rain gauge

You can make a rain gauge and actually find out how much rain falls in your area.

You will need:

- an open tin can
- an open box
- some sand

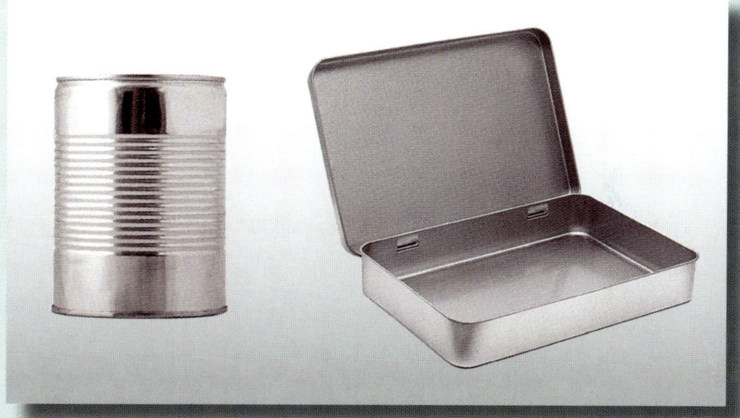

1. Set a lidless tin can in a box of sand. Make sure that the tin can is steady.
2. Place it in the open when it rains. There should be no obstacles to hinder the raindrops from falling into the tin.
3. After the rainfall, measure the water in the can. How many millimetres is it?

Weather Phenomena

Snow

When a cloud is very cold its water droplets freeze into ice crystals and come down as *snow*. At the earth's polar ice caps, it is so cold that water always falls to the ground as snow.

As ice crystals fall, they collide with each other to make patterned snowflake shapes. No two snowflake shapes are ever alike.

You too can make frost

Sometimes, water vapour in the air condenses directly into solid form. In below freezing temperatures, vapour condenses into frost on the cold pipes of a refrigerator. *Frost* is a covering of tiny crystals of ice that forms on cold surfaces.

You will need:

- a tall tin
- some ice cubes
- salt

1. Fill the tin with alternate layers of ice and salt. The ice should be twice the amount of salt.
2. Now observe what happens to the outside of the tin. You have frost!

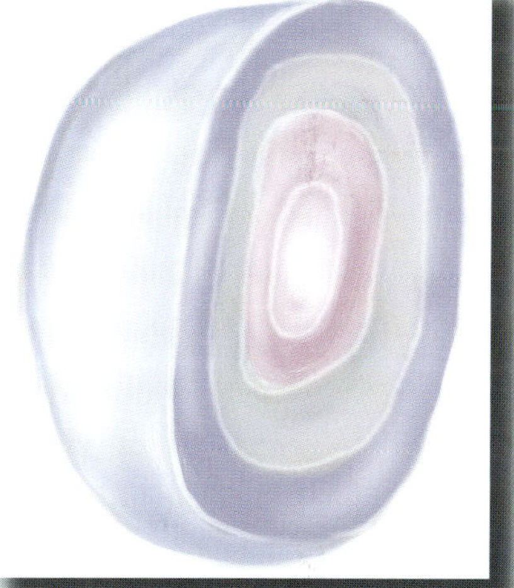

Hailstones begin as tiny ice pellets in high clouds. They gradually grow bigger as water freezes on them. A hailstone is made up of lots of frozen layers, almost like an onion.

Fog forms on cold, still nights when the cold ground chills the air above it. The vapour in the air condenses into a cloud of fine water droplets.

Storms

Storms occur when the air is hot and humid. It rises and forms thunderclouds in the sky. Electricity builds up in thunder clouds and is released as lightning. A lightning flash heats up the air in its path, and the air expands quickly, making a booming clap of thunder. Thunder and lightning occur simultaneously, but we see the lightning first because light travels faster than sound.

Around 2,000 thunderstorms occur in the world at any one given time.

Monsoons

A monsoon is a seasonal wind. It blows from the sea to the land in summers, and from the land to the sea in winter. In lands near the equator, the air grows very hot in summer. It expands and thins out. Cooler and denser air from the sea is sucked inland. This air carries a lot of moisture. This moisture falls as torrential rain so vital to the growth of crops. In India, the monsoon lasts for three to four months.

Droughts

However, the monsoon is not predictable — sometimes too much rain brings flood and sometimes the rains fail, causing a drought. During a drought, plants and crops die from lack of rain, causing great hardships and starvation to the local people.

Can scientists make rain?

Droughts (lack of rain) are a serious problem in many parts of the world. Scientists have tried 'seeding' clouds with crystals of carbon dioxide, either from a rocket or an aircraft. The crystals act like natural ice particles in clouds, around which tiny water droplets gather to form raindrops. Another method is to release silver iodide smoke into the atmosphere. However, no scientist has yet made rain fall from a cloudless sky!

Telling about the Weather

Scientists who study weather are called *meteorologists*. They use different instruments like the windvane, thermometer, anemometer, rain gauge and barometer to keep track of the following things:

- the temperature of the air
- the direction and speed of the wind
- the changing air pressure
- moisture in the air
- the clouds
- the amount of rainfall

There are weather satellites going round the earth. Their cameras take pictures of clouds, the land, ice in the sea storms, tornadoes and hurricanes. This information helps weather forecasters know about the weather.

A network of five satellites called 'metstats' provide a weather-watch for the whole world. You can often see metstat pictures on television weather forecasts.

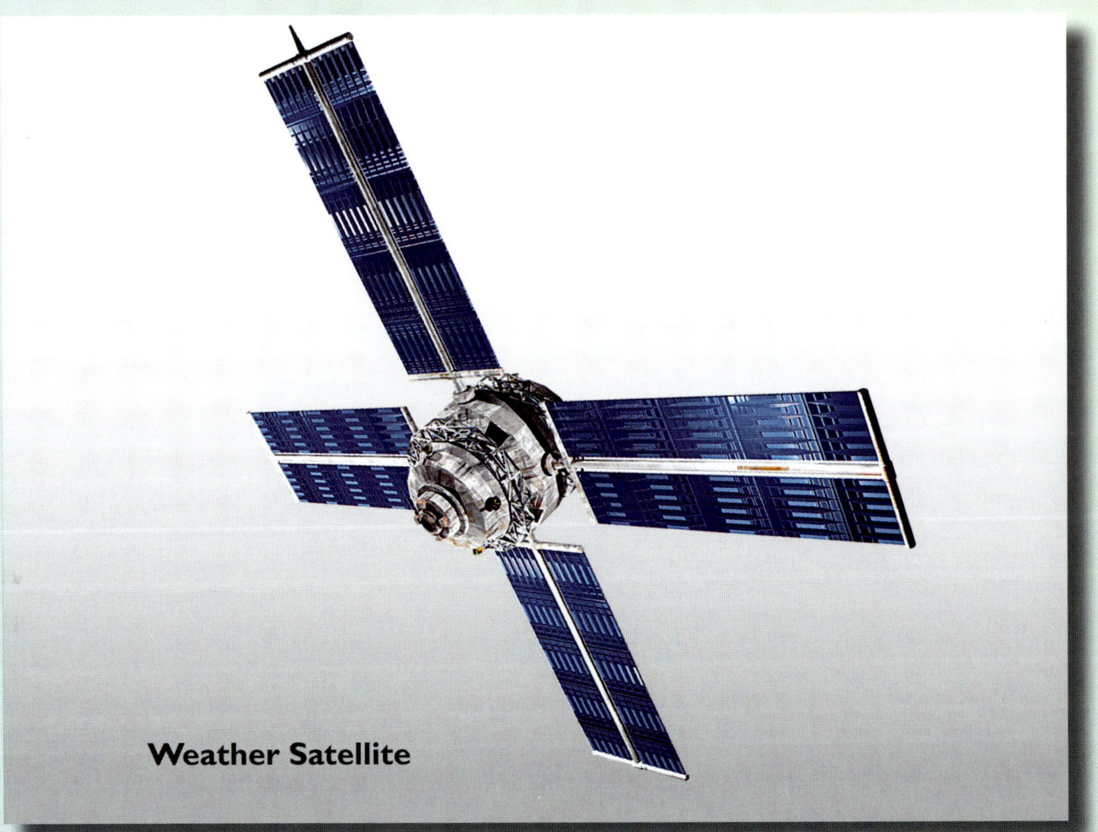

Weather Satellite

Weather maps

Weather forecasters make use of all the information they gather to make weather maps.

HI: 61

LO: 51

Weather stations all over the world report to one large weather bureau. The weather bureau tells sailors on ships, pilots on aeroplanes, farmers and other people about the weather.

Man-made Weather Changes

Sometimes weather is changed accidentally by the pollution caused by mankind. In some big cities smoke from factories and power stations, and vehicle exhaust fumes mix with fog to form 'smog', which is dirty and dangerous to breathe.

Harmful chemicals from factories and cars can also mix with water vapour in the air to produce acid rain. Acid rain may kill plants, make lakes unfit for fish and gradually eat into metal and buildings.

What is the greenhouse effect?

The fuels we burn, in cars, houses, power stations and factories give off carbon dioxide. This builds up as a layer in the atmosphere. Heat from the sun is normally reflected back from the earth and most of it bounces back into space. However, the thickening layer of carbon dioxide acts like glass in a greenhouse, trapping the heat inside. Scientists believe that the 'greenhouse effect' could, by warming the planet, change the weather in some parts of the world.